MW01378352

MRS. KETNER

TALKS ABOUT

MENTAL HEALTH

AMY KETNER

Copyright © 2024 Amy Ketner
All rights reserved
First Edition

PAGE PUBLISHING
Conneaut Lake, PA

First originally published by Page Publishing 2024

ISBN 979-8-89157-848-7 (pbk)
ISBN 979-8-89157-850-0 (digital)

Printed in the United States of America

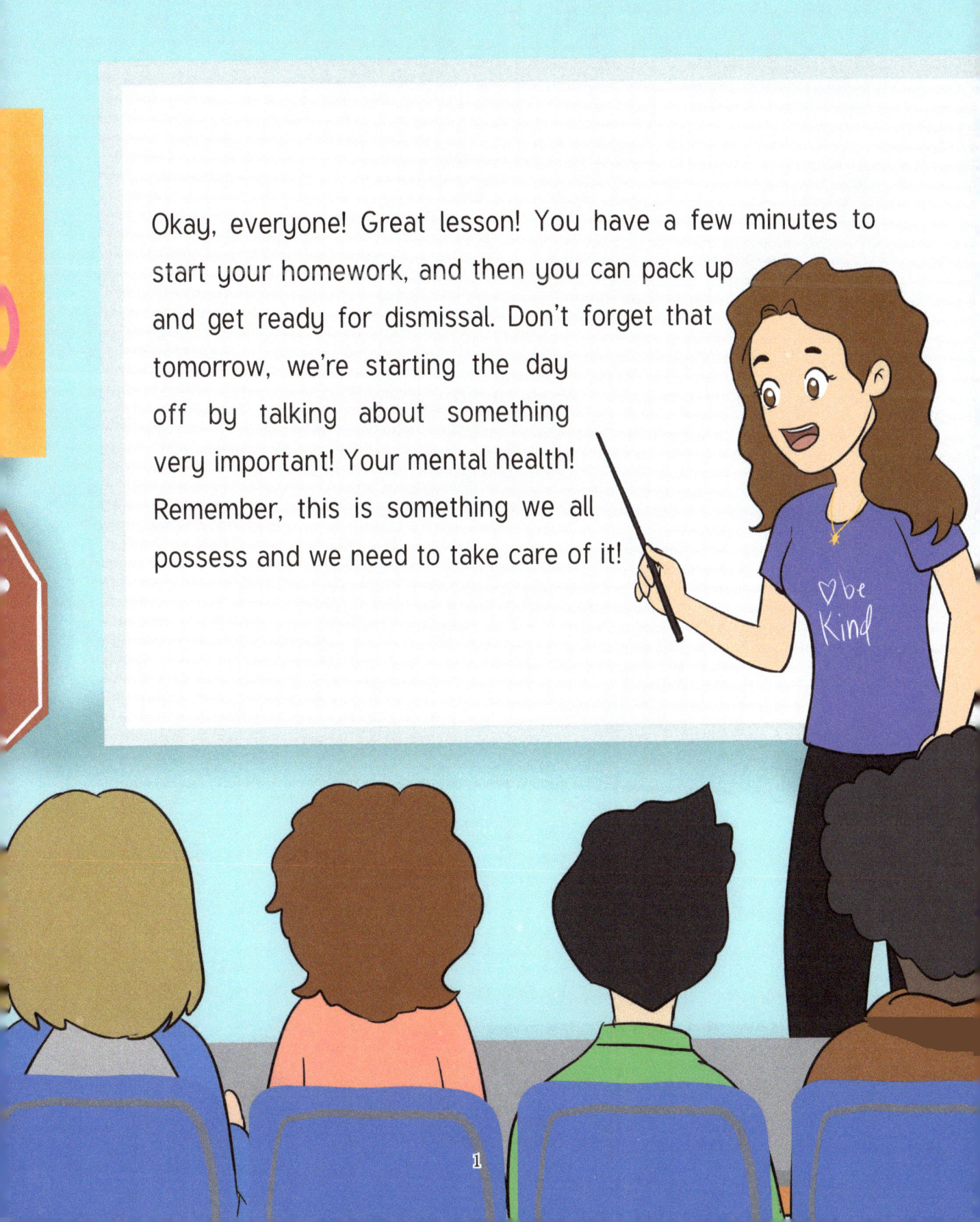

Okay, everyone! Great lesson! You have a few minutes to start your homework, and then you can pack up and get ready for dismissal. Don't forget that tomorrow, we're starting the day off by talking about something very important! Your mental health! Remember, this is something we all possess and we need to take care of it!

Psst...hey, Kath...what is this mental health, and how does Mrs. Ketner know that I possess it? Oh man! Is this something Mrs. Ketner passed out at the beginning of the school year, and now she thinks we still have it? I can't find the class pet I took home with me two weeks ago! How does she think I'm still going to have something from the beginning of the school year?

What? Why would you do that? Homework is for *home*...hello! It even has the word *home* in it! Anyway...back to my question... where is your mental health? Where did you put it? Maybe if you tell me where you put yours, I'll remember where I put mine!

Wait...did you just say you lost the class pet? I thought you told me you were taking good care of Joel the frog.

Relax...I'm leaving food and water out all over my house. He's fine! Now seriously, Kathie! I need you to focus! Where did you put your mental health? In your dresser? Closet? Under your bed? In your diary that's on your nightstand under all those books...by the way, why do you read so much?

I like to read! It's good for your mind! Wait! how do you know about my books and where my diary is? Oh, never mind! I don't know where you put your mental health, but I know exactly where mine is, and I take good care of it! Now let me be so I can work on my homework!

Girls, there's a lot of talking back there. Do you need something?

No, sorry, Mrs. Ketner. I was just telling Kathie she could start her homework now if she wants, even though *home* is in the word, it's okay to start it at school.

Good luck finding your mental health! Maybe it's with Joel the Frog somewhere!

School bell rings.

Have a great night, everyone! See you tomorrow morning! Don't forget we're talking about mental health tomorrow. Super important topic, so make sure you're here!

Ugh! Where is my mental health? Did I pack it away with my summer clothes that my mom made me pack up last weekend?

Did I bury it in the backyard when I hid my time capsule? Did I accidentally wash it away when I was helping my dad wash his car?

Sherri...why are you making an even bigger mess than usual? Let me guess, you lost something...*again*?

Umm...I don't know what that's supposed to mean, but I may have just misplaced something, but I'm sure it'll turn up... somewhere!

(Sherri texting Kathie) Hey, Kath...it's me, your best bud, Sherri! I can't find my mental health anywhere! Can you please help me find it?

Oh, hey, Sherri...I'm working on my homework, since you know, the word *home* is in it! Okay, okay...I can't help you find it, but I'll give you a hint that might help you! You didn't put it anywhere, and from what I know of you, you actually take pretty good care of your mental health!

Thanks, I think, but I didn't put it anywhere, and I take good care of it? Well, that makes no sense!

Okay...if I was mental health...where would I be? Hmm...okay...
maybe if I do some singing and dancing, I'll remember! That always
helps me when I'm feeling a little stressed out!

Sherri, it's time for dinner!

Thanks, Mom! This looks delicious and so healthy! Mmm...

It sounded like you did a lot of dancing and singing...lots of *loud* singing!

Yep! Dancing and singing really make me feel good inside! It's just like when I draw, read, take a rest, or do brownie breathing with Mrs. Ketner. I can't really explain it, but I like the way I feel after I do it, especially if I have a stressful day like today!

Oh no! You had a stressful day?

Yeah, kind of! I just...well...Mrs. Ketner said we all have this really important thing, and I don't know where mine is! I think you were right! I think I lost it! I'm really sorry, Mom! I know I tend to lose or misplace things all the time! Can you please help me find it?

Oh, honey, thanks for telling me! I hope you feel better that you shared that with me! Tell me what you lost, and we'll see if we can find it.

I do feel better talking about it, that's for sure, but I lost... well...I lost my mental health!

Oh, Sherri! You didn't lose it! You have mental health in your body! Mental health is how we think, feel, and act. It helps us deal with our stress, how to make good choices, and how to get along with others. Mental health even helps us deal with stressful days, like today! Your mental health is just as important as your physical health!

So what you're saying is that I didn't lose it! I've had it the whole time?

Yes, indeed! And you do a great job taking care of your mental health!

Really?

Yes, all the things you do like dancing, listening to music, singing, getting enough sleep, limiting screen time, reading, drawing, brownie breathing with Mrs. Ketner, and even resting all help your mental health! And, having good friends like Kathie to laugh and talk with also helps support your mental health! Oh! I almost forgot, even taking care of a pet can help your mental health! So it's great that you're taking care of Joel the frog!

Wow! I didn't know all those things about mental health! Thanks, Mom! I, uh, I better go and get my bath and get to bed! I'm sure taking care of my body and getting enough sleep are also really important for my mental health!

Yes! You got it now! Go ahead, you can be excused from the table to start all of that!

Thanks, Mom!

Here, Joel...here, boy! Come on, buddy! Stop playing hide and go seek!

Finally! I get to sit down and relax! Uh, Sherri...why is Joel sitting on our couch?

Oh! I told him to get some rest. You know, take care of his mental health!

Good morning, class! Let's start our morning by doing our brownie breathing. Picture in your head a big pan of warm, ooey-gooey brownies coming out of the oven! Inhale through your nose, breathe in the warm, delicious smell of brownies, and then slowly exhale the air out through your mouth and cool the brownies off! Let's do it two more times! Great job getting your brain and body ready for the day! Remember I said we're going to talk about mental health today? Who knows what mental health is? Sherri! Thanks for volunteering!

Mental health is how we think, feel, and act. It helps us deal with our stress, helps us make good choices, and helps us to get along with others. We can take care of our mental health by exercising, singing loudly to our favorite songs, taking rests, and hanging out with good friends, like Kathie!

Wow! I'm impressed! That's exactly right! Great job, Sherri!

Mrs. Ketner, if we have good mental health, can we also have bad mental health?

Oh, Kathie, you're always one step ahead of me! It must be all those books you read! Well, to answer your question, we don't have bad mental health. We might have bad days, but taking care of our mental health every day will help with those bad days! And if anyone ever feels like they're having more bad days than good days, you can talk to an adult like me, who can help with that! The important thing is to never feel embarrassed or bad about talking about your mental health!

Sherri, why did Joel just jump out of your bookbag?

Oh! Well because I know that taking care of a pet also helps your mental health, so I thought someone else might want to take care of Joel and their mental health all at the same time!

Reflection Questions

1. What is mental health?
2. List all of the ways Sherri takes care of her mental health.
3. Who is someone you can talk to when you're feeling stressed?
4. Draw a picture of how you take care of your mental health.

ABOUT THE AUTHOR

 Amy Ketner was born and raised in the Coal Region of Schuylkill County, Pennsylvania. Although her family faced struggles and Amy was bullied in high school, she always had a strong support network including family, friends, and teachers. She has kept her great sense of humor, and although it's changed quite a few times, her amazing curly hair got her through it all! It's because Amy focused on the positive experiences that she knew her mission in life was to encourage and help children with challenges they may face growing up. Amy has over twenty-five years of counseling experience, eighteen of those years in school counseling, and she is the founder of Kid and Play Yoga..

Printed in the USA
CPSIA information can be obtained
at www.ICGtesting.com
CBHW061955130724
11387CB00037B/664

9 798891 578487